Understanding the War We Are in Today

Understanding the War We Are in Today

Martin J. Blickstein

WORTHY SHORTS™
New York

Published by Worthy Shorts™
The On-Line Private Press for Professionals

ISBN 978-1-935340-14-0
WS108

Worthy Shorts™ is a registered trademark.

Print version manufactured in the
United States of America

For more information, visit
www.WorthyShorts.com

MY BOOK, "Anticipating Tomorrow" describes the manner in which technology impacts the nontechnological world. Being in the 9th decade of my life with a ticking clock, I am not surprised by the clash of civilizations engendered by those transformations nor by the passion of the subsequent confrontations, of which Al Queda is a prime example. We call the people battling for modernity a "national army". They call theirs an "army of God". That dichotomy may seem a huge simplification but it goes straight to the heart of the issues.

Our opponents can legitimately claim as much as 1/5 of the world's population as potential recruits. With such a fragmented antagonist who would we negotiate with? What would constitute victory with such a splintered adversary and how does one get all of them to recognize it?" "Who signs the peace treaty, and indeed can there be a general peace treaty?" Considering the nature of our opposition, it isn't even off subject to ask how industrial powers that design and produce GPS guided missiles can defeat preindustrial polyglots many of whom still produce mostly opium, carpets and slaves and whom still deliver their "products" by camel?

The wars I have observed had an identifiable beginning and end. This one doesn't. The conflicts I am familiar with have identifiable goals on both sides. This one doesn't. The wars of my generation were between nations. This one isn't. Our wars were fought between uniformed armies. This one isn't. In my wars, religion was the excuse, not the reason. Religion is the fundamental, if not the only, rationale for this one. With all of those differences, it should be interesting to identify the distinctions and their consequences. It doesn't take much time to realize that the variance is based on a very long Muslim history which is quite divergent from that of Europe and for a profoundly fundamental reason. Most of the world's populations are separated by water, by land, by mountains, or by boundaries. The separations can be bridged by armies and tradesmen on horseback, in cars, in ships, or even by foot. The Middle East, outside of the Fertile Crescent, is separated by sand. It is not in banter that the camel is called the "ship of the desert".

Historically, villages grew around oases and were isolated from each other, even if only by a few miles of sand. In Europe, the original settlement was the "citystate". In deserts, it was the village state. The description of "nationhood" was a fiction attributed to them by the West. Agriculture was ubiquitous everywhere in the world. Desert people live by trade and/or by war. (Slaves were a major commercial "product") At the height of its power, the Ottoman "Empire" was barely more than a paste up of settlements which more or less shared a religion but little else. Indeed, one of the Prophets' major goals was to stop the endless tribal wars. The Muslim world never experienced a Reformation as did the West. The Sunni's and the Shia's are still fighting battles that started nearly 1400 years ago. This chronicle is one of the impelling factors in President Bush's failing war in Iraq and it continues to be a major aspect of the ancient inability of Muslims to accept any grating "outsiders" in their midst.

If one were to judge from the amount of print space and broadcast time devoted to the socalled Middle-East these days, it might be easy to picture an enormous number of residents. Actually, it is a relatively small settled area with relatively few people. Its obvious importance derives from its history as being the origin of modern civilization (while until recently, as we shall see, refusing to join the rest of the world) and its major resource —oil. They seem to be floating on a sea of underground oil— over 50% of the worlds' known reserves. A small part of this region is called the Fertile Crescent and is purported to be the original location of the Garden of Eden and is definitely the land of origin of the Abrahamic religions —Hebrew, Christian, and Muslim.

Many Jews like to think that "they were in the area first" but, in fact, there were people in the area before them and even the Old Testament supports that thesis. The Old Testament reports that God gave them rights to this land (the called "Caanan") and instructed them (the Hapiruo to evict the residents (the Hittites, the Philistines, the Mycenaens, and even some Greeks). More likely, modern Jews descended from the then residents but the details are lost in a history almost 40 centuries old. In any case, this people have had a stormy history ever since. The Assyrians conquered Israel in 722 BC and the Babylonians conquered Judah around 586 BC (both part of what came to be known as "Judea" —parts of the Hebrew "inheritance") The Babylonians, fearful of Jewish numbers, exiled them from their homeland. Fifty years later the Persian King Cyrus conquered the Babylonians and permitted the Jews to return to their homeland. Pushed from pillar to post all over the world from then till now, the most significant feature in their history is that after 40 centuries of migration with no "nationality" and no regional cultural center of gravity, they survived to this day as a recognizable but constantly fearful ethnic people.

The Zionist movement (i.e., the "return") is actually fairly new although there had always been many resident Jews in Palestine. Zionism became a formal organization in 1897. It was founded by Theodor Herzl with the first Zionist Congress taking place in Switzerland. They developed farm communities and even cities such as Tel Aviv. By 1914, with a total Palestine population of about 700,000, about 100,000 were Jews. During WWI, the British would promise anything to anyone to buy loyalty and the Sykes-Picot Agreement of 1916 appears to have promised the same land to a number of "allies" including the Jews, the Turks, the Arabs, and even the Russians and therein lies at least some of the initial blame for the Palestinian/Israeli conflict. that goes on to this day.

Jesus Christ was born in the Judean town of Bethlehem during a period of great turmoil when the Hebrews were trying to shed Roman hegemony. By this time, Judea was a colony of Rome and was being ruled by the Herod family who, like the Babylonians before them, exiled the Jews from the land although the area continued to have a large Jewish population many of whom converted to the new religion founded by Jesus. It offered hope at a time when hope was absent from their lives.

During the seventh century AD, a third great prophet was born in this area. His name was Muhammad. His message was so appealing to the local population that within 50 years his religion had spread all over the Middle East. The Jewish message never spread at all, but then they didn't want it to spread. The Christian message took many centuries. The Muslim message took 50 years. Historically, there was every reason in the world to expect the ultimate victory of Islam over Europe. In the beginning it was the Arabs who were making the social and military advances. The early Abbasids (around 780—) were actually famous because the era was one of unrivaled intellectual activity – science, history, literature, technology including the life of the Prophet himself. Such a progressive leadership soon vanished in the fratricidal conflict between the Sunni's and the Shia.

Off and on, the Muslims dominated the area for over a thousand years with many interruptions, such as the Crusades in the 12th century. In 1099, the Crusaders captured Jerusalem and Jaffa where these latter day followers of Jesus initiated a slaughter of both the Jewish and the Muslim inhabitants that is famous for its ferocity to this day. Jerusalem was retaken by the Muslims in the year 1187 and they have remained there since then.

A thousand years later, Europe was actually bounded by Islam for three centuries— on the south, the east and the steppe, with only ice in the north and water on the west. At the same time Islam extended over three continents. Within one half century after the Prophet's death, Islam was a world religion with one language, one culture, and a remarkable scientific establishment. During the time that Europe was seriously trying to determine how many angels would fit on the head of a pin, Islam was developing a number system which subsequently became the standard of the entire world. While Europe was burning its astronomers at the stake, Islam's astronomers were trying to determine how many planets constituted our planetary system. When Paris was still a village on the Seine River, Constantinople was a city. When Europe's few intellectuals were vitally interested in Islamic culture, the Moslems felt, with some justification for a time, that Europe's culture had nothing to offer them. (Interestingly, there never was an Arabic dictionary.)

It was a Moslem universality that "To permit what God forbids is no less a sin than to forbid what God allows". That simple statement made all European culture superfluous. The question of the Muslim resident in non-Muslim countries was rarely referred to while the reverse was common because the Muslim influence was, at that time constantly expanding. This fact left the Ottomans with a serious problem when their influence began to wane leaving many of their number resident elsewhere.

Were it not for the Shia attempt to dominate the Ottoman Empire and its masses (who were largely Sunni) from within, Europe might well have been overrun by the Muslims in the 16th century. The Ottomans, mostly Sunni's, never settled with the Persians, mostly Shia, never triumphed even in Spain (which soon became rich and aggressive due to the wealth coming from the New World. Interestingly, the New World gold ultimately defeated Spanish ambitions as well. There was so much of it that they had no need to develop their home industry and science because they (the Spanish) could buy whatever they wanted or needed. One of their major purchases turned out to be the Catholic Church, in gratitude for God's beneficence in leading them to America. As it turned out, they would have been better off investing in Science and Industry.)

Still, there were European inroads in the Middle East culture and economy. The first non-official newspaper in Turkey appeared as early as 1840. The Crimean war in 1854 was the first victory of Muslims over Europeans (The Crimean War lasted from 1854 until 1856 and was fought between Imperial Russia on one side with an alliance of the United Kingdom, France, the Kingdom of Sardinia, and the Ottoman Empire on the other), and further expanded the interest. Furthermore, the Arabs, even under the rule of the Ottomans, were never a unified nation and had no sense of "nation". Each village lived essentially as a tribe usually on or near an oasis, with its own "army". The major influence that the Ottoman Empire had was in the bigger towns. Outside of the towns, the local sheikh ruled and commanded his own militia. By 1914, only 5% of collected taxes ever reached the Ottoman Government. In Egypt and Cypress the Sheikhdoms were under British influence. Lebanon was ruled by a Christian military governor and even the Porte, i.e., the Ottoman capital, was governed in consultation with 6 European powers. And everywhere in the middle-east, Russia and France reserved the right to defend Orthodox & Catholic populations.

The Ottoman Empire was clannish and tribal with little cohesion anywhere, even including the towns. In total, however, it was considerably more populous than

Europe. By the 16th century the Empire included the Middle East, North Africa, the Bosporus and Europe from the Persian Gulf to the Danube, including Hungary, Bulgaria, Yugoslavia, Hertsogovena and Bosnia. The Empire was estimated at 35 million people. By way of comparison, contemporary Great Britain was probably 4 million. Eventually the Empire retreated from North Africa, Europe, and Hungary. The major source of Ottoman opulence was captured wealth and slaves. Over the centuries, they had mastered the art of warfare, never governance. Amazingly, in retrospect, the Ottomans were never a productive empire but, somehow, Europe never figured that out until after WWII.

In the West, the misjudgment was so extensive that the entire Allied war effort of WWI was misguided by it. As an example, Kitchener believed this misinformation to the extent that he was convinced that the entire Moslem world was a single entity with unified leadership. In fact they were so disorganized that the Porte (located in Turkey, of course) ordered the construction of a battleship in England and subsequently found that they couldn't take delivery because there was no port in Turkey adequate to dock the ship. The Germans were similarly misguided. After the WWI started, the Germans found, to their dismay, that the Turks could not come to their (the German's) assistance because the they had no transportation facilities. As another example, the British commander of the Middle East army sent his troops marching all the way to Baghdad (April, 1915). The effort required troop conveyance, medical supplies, munitions, etc., but there were no roads, no rails nor any other vehicles. They had to literally walk and use camels. The British army initially did achieve a pyrrhic victory but could not sustain their effort due to the total lack of mobility. They were being decimated by bands of disconnected locals and they began a forced retreat (November, 1915) which was such a disaster that they suffered over 10,000 casualties and had to dispatch 23,000 troops to rescue the survivors. The rescue was billed in British papers as a great victory.

Wartime Britain was also alarmed by a rumor that the Arabs (i.e., the Ottomans) were planning an "Arabia for Arabs" movement to oust the Europeans. The Ottomans were so disjointed that the "movement" could never be initiated. The rumor was sufficiently disturbing that the British, in an effort to head off this development, planned to offer "Islam" the establishment of a Moslem nation which would be headquartered in Mecca and/or Medina as compensation for the defeat and dismemberment of the Ottoman Empire.

The effort in the Middle East heavily engaged Winston Churchill, and included so many mistakes and missed opportunities that it led a conservative newspaper, reviewing the process of WWI, to editorialize that "there is some tragic flaw in Churchill's character which determines him on every occasion in the wrong course". Interestingly, there was one major player who has never been accorded due honor. Her name was Gertrude Bell. She was the daughter of a very wealthy English family which founded huge chemical and aluminum industries. She was awarded a first-class degree in modern history at Oxford and was the very first woman in British history to achieve the rank of "officer of the military intelligence service". She was a very real power broker of the Ottoman Empire after the WWI breakup of that empire and was described as "the incarnation of the emancipated heiress who used her money to buy opportunity for service, not privilege". She was almost consistently correct in her analysis while Winston Churchill was almost consistently wrong, yet the name remembered, for whatever reason, was that of Churchill.

After the defeat of the Ottomans, the peace conference included over 10,000 participating people with their separate and personal agendas and ambitions. Small wonder. They had to deal with a truly dizzying array of agreements, official and not so official, which were sometimes paradoxical, typically ambiguous, more often conflicting, and almost uniformly clashing. These "agreements" included, but were certainly not limited to:

The Constantinople Agreement 1915
The Treaty of London 1915
The McMahon Agreement 1916
The Sykes Picot Agreement 1916
The Balfour Declaration 1917
The Hogarth Message 1915
The Declaration of Seven 1918
The Anglo-French Declaration 1918
Wilson's 14 Points 1918
The Four Ends 1918
The Five Particulars 1918

And that's only a sample.

The British thought they had unloaded the problem Middle-East areas while acquiring the peaceful areas themselves. That soon unraveled with vengeance. In 1918, The Egyptians demanded independence followed almost immediately by Afghanistan and Iraq. In 1919, the (Saudi) Arabians claimed independence. All over the Middle-East, the Moslems acted alike but never in concert. Even the Kurdish areas, with basically tribal people scattered over the plateaus and mountains in the north of Iraq, Iran, Armenia, and Turkey, fought as detached gorilla groups in the face of their majority in Kurdistan (about seven million population— mostly Sunni).

In 1920, the Arab Jewish conflict exploded. The other allies had their own troubles. In 1920, the French had a major conflict with Syria while the Russians faced Moslem revolts almost everywhere. And then there was the ever growing problem of Zionism. The British had very mixed feelings about a Jewish state – indeed about Jews in general. Some few, like General Allenby, were positive about such a state.

The main Jewish proponent, Dr. Weizmann, wanted to cooperate with resident Arabs by having Jews buy land not then in use. Weizmann's plan, presented to Feisal (later King Feisal) was almost legendary in its simplicity. The plan reduced to:

1. The settlers were to avoid encroaching on land then in use.
2. The land owners had an open market for land sales. (Ultimately they wound up selling land to the settlers at 40 to 80 times the original purchase price. Considering that this was mostly land abandoned because it was overcropped, that had to be the celebration to end all celebrations by the foreign landowners. As a matter of record,

at least 25% of the land owners had, in fact, already sold land to the Jews between 1920 and 1928 so further selling was hardly a radical move.

The majority of the landowners were not even local Arabs. They were Egyptians and Turks who made a very handsome profit selling land they had previously rented at usurious rates to Bedouins who would disappear when the land lost its fertility.

The Jews were generally resident population and émigrés from East Europe all of whom had the advantage of financing from Europe and America. Unlike the common perception, those original "Zionists" were secular, not religious Jews. Harassment by Moslem neighbors was a fairly common occurrence, usually provoked by local Sheikhs, but after WWI, those attacks became concerted. In 1919 Bedouin tribes attacked Jewish settlements all over the Galilee with untypical coordination. In 1920, the violence became so pronounced that the Jewish settlers formed a "defense legion" in response to the clear failure of the British to provide even superficial protection.

Lloyd George tried to back his promise to the Jews by disbanding the British Military Administration and appointing Hersholt Samuel as head of a new civilian administration. The violence continued, secretly encouraged and even organized by Winston Churchill, by now no enthusiast of a Jewish homeland. Churchill was convinced that the British commitment to the Zionists would be satisfied by an independent Arab state no further west than the Jordan River and a separate Arab entity east of the river. The consensus among the "Arab British" (i.e., pro-Arab British administrators) was that the area could support as many as ten times the population of 1920 considering the recognized enterprise of the Zionists and the unrestricted right of unlimited Jewish settlement in Palestine became the fundamental issue of debate among the British "administrators".

The ultimate Middle-East political "settlement" was signed in 1922 reflecting the same demonstrably confused and conflicting purpose demonstrated by the Allies going into WWI in the first place. It produced "nations" and boundaries where none had ever previously existed and attempted to sell legitimacy thereof (as for instance, Jordan, Iraq, Iran, and Palestine). Life in the post World War I. Middle-East became very tenuous for the Jewish residents. In fact, it wasn't all that good for the Muslim residents.

The WWI peace treaty had established the kingdom of Jordan with the Husseini family as its head. The Husseini's nonchalantly killed both Jews and Arabs opposed to the hegemony. Most of all, the agreement tried to install "democracy" in a area that had never distinguished between church and state with leaders in such disrepute that local wars and revolts broke out the day after the agreements were signed. In an area whose only customs were based on Quran and "Sharia", the peace agreement attempted to install secular governments. This agreement marked the climax of the centuries old European effort to colonize the world.

Into this world, the U.N introduced yet another anomaly, the Jewish state of Israel in November of 1947. The Jews accepted both the UN decision and the geographic boundaries of the new nation as defined by the UN. The Arabs rejected it. At this time there were about 600,000 Jews in Palestine, almost all in the area assigned to Israel by the UN with probably twice that many Arabs. Jerusalem was to be internationalized. The day after partition was announced, it was evident that it would not work.

During the time before Israeli independence was announced there are already two Arab armies of "independents" operating , one led by El Husseini in the Jerusalem area and other by El Kaukji in the Galilee. As is cutomary with the Arabs, their armies acted in conjunction but not in concert. Most of the Arab states which joined the war did so reluctantly for fear of an Arab victory without their participation. The Jews on the other hand, were very much coordinated. Major action broke out in Jerusalem, Haifa, Gush Etzion, Deir Yassin, along with almost countless smaller engagements everywhere. Arab Palestinians began leaving their homes, particularly in the larger towns such as Haifa, by April of 1948 in spite of appeals by both Jewish and British officials to remain. Despite initial Arab victories, the Jews, with better coordination and better military intelligence won decisively.

By the end of the war in 1949, the Jews had substantially expanded the boundaries set by the UN. As much as 78% of the West Bank was now in Israeli hands, as well as all of Jerusalem. Over 700,000 Arabs had fled Israel to become refugees in Arab countries which, to this day, have not accepted their presence. With their very large reproduction rate, those refugee camps are now home to millions of Palestinians. Alternatively, all Jewish refugees from anywhere, including the Arab countries, were integrated into the Israeli population within days of their arrival in Israel.

The war, in fact, never ended and continues to this day with major and minor events. The vocalized demand of the Arabs was the "right of return" –i.e., that all displaced Palestinians be permitted to return to their homes in

Israel. That would produce an Arab majority in Israel within a single generation. The Israeli demand was to retain all new settlements and several key strategic areas of the West Bank. The most central demand of the Israelis was the requirement that the Arabs drop the intention of destroying the state of Israel from their stated goal and the Arab refusal to comply. In December of 2000, American President Clinton made a proposal which purportedly returned 97% of the territory of the West Bank as well as sovereignty of West Bank airspace. Saudi Ambassador Prince Bandar said "If Arafat does not accept what is available now, it won't be a tragedy, it will be a crime". Clinton stated that Arafat had made a colossal blunder and there has been no significant negotiations since then. (the PLO has denied the Clinton statements regarding Taba.) In 2001, the Israelis made further concessions, which were once again refused.) By now it was clear that the Arabs had no intention of dropping their ambition of destroying the state of Israel and the Israelis had no intention of dismantling the settlements unless and until the Arabs dropped their goal..

Major fighting flared in 1956, 1967 as well as 1973. There were countless other satellite engagements including Lebanon in 1975 and 1982 and in Jordan. Failing to win any national military engagements, the

Arabs returned to their traditionally successful local battle plan, i.e., individual actions not necessarily coordinated with any "master plan" or central strategy. In the beginning this strategy was called "intifada". It was the type of warfare which disabled organized enemy armies and minimized enemy technical advantages. It was the effective strategy which had defeated the Romans, the Crusaders, the Russians, the Europeans, and, it was hoped, would ultimately defeat the Zionists. It was a tactic which forced well equipped, easily identifiable troops to fight comparatively poorly armed civilians who would melt back into the population after each action, putting the unformed armies in the position of attacking "innocent civilians" or not defending themselves.

From all of this mess there emerged an unscripted glimmer of hope, after more than a half century of failed hopes. In the "Geneva Accords" a number of well known Israeli opposition leaders, in cooperation with well known Palestinian leaders announced an agreement in principle which came to be known as the "Geneva Accord". In essence the Israeli side would surrender sovereignty of Arab sections of Jerusalem and the Arabs would renounce the right of return. The agreement drew praise and support from many of the world's leaders including Colin Powell and Yasser Arafat. While the agreement has no official standing, it sits there and stares at the belligerents. Both sides are actively trying to torpedo it. At the moment, nothing else is on the table beyond such desperate measures as walling off the West Bank and the Gaza, a measure which would effectively lose more West Bank Arab land, cut off even more Arabs from their jobs, and encourage more chaos and corruption in the Palestinian territories.

And so, in this part of the Middle East, where everything is always in flux, there continues to be no change in the basic positions of both sides. The Palestinians continue to use the ancient Muslim strategy of disjointed chaos and ruin while the Israelis continue to use their massive military power to respond overwhelmingly, but futilely. Americans and Europeans have vowed never to actively engage either side until the Arabs abandon their ambition of destroying Israel and Israel abandons the settlements. Both of them wouldn't budge from those specific positions. As long as those conditions prevail, all their other "negotiations" are merely window dressing for the audience but it adds additional instability to a vital area of the world which monopolizes the supply of the one commodity which is vital to the entire industrial world. That commodity is oil. And the "also ran" feature of this show now shifted.

Iraq was another glued together outcome of WWI. On September 11, 2001 four airliners filled with passengers and loaded with fuel, were hijacked with three of them successfully being flown into their targets. (The fourth one crashed, thanks to passenger heroism.) This was another example that a major industrial power with overwhelming military capacity could be successful challenged by activists who lacked even a national home base, had no army, no real central leadership, no industrial capacity, and even lacked widespread support from the very Muslims which supposedly constituted their "base". It wasn't very hard to trace the source back to Al Qaeda and Bin Laden. Al Qaeda had a well identified training camp in Afghanistan which the leadership of Afghanistan refused to terminate. This time the ancient strategy of disjointed attacks would not work because there was an identifiable target which an organized army could eliminate, and we did, with the approval of virtually every country in the world – at least initially.

However, before the Afghan war was complete, the United States moved its sights to another Muslim target. On March 20, 2003, American, British, and Australian troops invaded Iraq based on the much publicized premise of "preemption"— i.e., we would attack them before they could attack us. U.S. forces entered Baghdad on

April 29, a military feat which astonished the entire Muslim world because the Iranians essentially lost their war against the Iraqis after three years of conflict. The Palestinians, with the ancient Muslim pattern of playing long odds, sided with Saddam Hussein. The American President, with much bravado and the orchestrated applause of an aircraft carrier, announced the successful end of the Iraqi war. It turned out to be a bit premature. Since his victory announcement the U.S. has lost over 3,000 dead with 23,000 wounded. The war in Iraq has turned the entire Middle East into a boiling cauldron with the British and Australians looking to exit the conflict. All of that with almost no major engagements. For the Americans, all the exit options are, at best, dismal and we are, after all the rhetoric, also trying find a way out.

Considering the ruinous consequences of the war, it is important to determine how we got into it. Was it accidental or deliberate? The sequence of events, with many supporting omissions can easily be summarized.

1999: Presidential candidate Bush tells his biographer (Mickey Herskowitz) that great leaders are only recognized when they are military commanders.

2000: Bush tells publisher Osama Siblani that if he is elected he will remove Saddam

Hussein and the Republican Party calls for a comprehensive plan to do so.

2000: Cheney publicly claims it might be necessary to remove Hussein by military means.

2001: Imam Sayed Hassan al Qazwini is told a number of times by Bush that he intends to remove Saddam Hussein

2001: A National Security Council meeting is told by Condi Rice that Iraq might be the key to reshaping the Middle East and that Saddam Hussein had to go. Paul O'Neill (Sec'y of the Treasury) claims "Why Saddam And Why Now" was never asked but the President instructed Pentagon officials to explore ways and means.

2001: The Washington Times reports that the Iraqi National Congress is negotiating a contract to train Iraqi expatriates for military work.

2001: Cheney's energy task force generates a series of documents outlining takeover procedures of the Iraqi oil fields.

2001: A report commissioned by the Council on Foreign Relations which recommends immediate policy reviews regarding Iraqi including military, energy, economic and political assessments.

2001: White House counterterrorism advisor Richard Clark meets with Bush,

Rumsfeld and Powell where Rumsfeld recommends bombing Iraq disregarding Powell's and Clark's warning that Iraq had nothing to do with 9/11. Clark later reports that Bush instructed him to "review" the evidence with the obvious purpose of tying Iraq into the 9/11 event.

2001: November. The USA Today reports that the decision to invade Iraq is made without the advice of any National Intelligence Estimate. Congressional pressure forces a review by the NIA but the declassified report issued to Congress omits key uncertainties.

2001: General Thomas Franks is instructed by Rumsfeld to work on war plans for Iraq

2001: Rumsfeld calls a secret meeting of the Defense Policy Board but does not invite Colin Powell. Most of Task Force 5's commandos in Afghanistan are pulled out to prepare for operations in Iraq in spite of the warning by CIA officials that invading Iraq will divert the fight against Al Qaeda at a crucial time as well as an admonition by the Egyptian President that an attack on Iraq can destabilize the entire Middle East.

2002: Key resources, such as intelligence personnel, munitions, and the spy planes which were intercepting Al Qaeda telephone calls are redirected away from Afghanistan to Iraq. The National Security Board is informed by the CIA that it is diverting key operations as well. Cheney is told by a number of Middle Eastern leaders that they will not support the Iraqi invasion.

2002: Arnaud de Borchgrave, the editor-at-large of the Washington Times, is told by neocons that the war against Iraq was never about WMD's. It was about reshaping the Middle East from the beginning. A reporter asks Bush if he has any concern about the war spreading hatred of the U.S. with more terrorist being created. He answers that we should not avoid taking action because irritated people might harm Americans.

Obviously this was a war of choice. Furthermore, it is now evident to virtually all the nations of the world that Saddam was being "contained" by our inspections, our air surveillance, and our commercial restrictions. In his January 2002 State of the Union address Bush pretty basically laid out his attitude and his policy when he announced, despite knowledge to the contrary, that "Time is not on our side. I will not wait on events while dangers gather. I will not stand by as peril draws closer and closer. The United States of

America will not permit the world's most dangerous regimes to threaten us with the world's most destructive weapons. In even further expansion of this fiction in June of 2002, he addressed the graduating class at the U.S. Military Academy at West Point, saying " Containment is not possible when unbalanced dictators with weapons of mass destruction can deliver those weapons on missiles or secretly provide them to terrorist allies. If we wait for threats to fully materialize, we will have waited too long......The only path to safety", he said, "is the path of action."

➤ On 9/7/02, Bush referred to an IAEA report purporting to say that Saddam was 6 months away from producing a nuclear weapon. No such report has ever been found.
➤ On 8/2/02, Cheney made two separate speeches predicting that Saddam will obtain nuclear weapons soon.
➤ On 10/7/02 Bush made a speech so riddled with false and misleading statements that one would need to reproduce the speech in its entirety to point them all out. Typical was his claim that Iraq has trained Al Qaeda personnel in bomb making and the production of poison gasses. Even the U.S. intelligence community disputed that

one. And, he claimed, Iraq had illegal Scud missiles. None were ever found.

As a matter of fact, Saddam's Iraq was so stripped of significant military capability that the UN debated the question of why he had risked so much to keep the inspectors out. Their final conclusion was that Saddam was obsessed with his image as this century's Saladin as well as his fear of becoming the target of his neighbors that he was hiding his martial incapacity from other Arabs, not from the UN. In retrospect, the inspections, the overflights, the UN restrictions on Iraq commerce, etc. with all the corruption, with all the ineptness, with all the inefficiencies, evidently did contain the dictator and immobilize him.

It seems pretty clear, even from this brief summary, that Bush intended to invade Iraq even before he was "elected", that Hussein's war making capacity contributed no part to Bush's decision to do so, that Bush did not foresee the human and the time and the financial cost of the war, that Bush had no knowledge nor any interest in Muslim history when he did make it and finally, that he did not anticipate any need for American activity after the war. It can also be inferred that his inept leadership of the war was ill served by a staff that should have been a great deal more competent than he was and a congress that should have been much more skeptical than it was.

In passing the "war resolution" many in Congress wanted a formal determination that further diplomacy "would not resolve the continuing threat", and that military action was demonstrably in response to terrorism including the 9/11 event. That determination was never forthcoming. Bush used the information which he provided to Congress to get the resolution passed and then cherry picked the resolution's referenced information (which he had provided in the first place) as reference for justification for military action. He continuously used the Powell report to the UN as "supporting documentation" in spite of Powell's evident reluctance at making the report, and even after that report had been proven to be generally false.

Chief of Staff General Zinni and a significant number of others on the DOD staff were against incursion but they didn't prevail. 9/11 provided the perfect excuse for invasion in spite of the absence of any postmilitary occupation plan and the vocal opposition of many of the more experienced Republican cadre including Bush Sr. (Brent Scowcroft, chairman of the Foreign Intelligence Advisory Board made the point most succinctly when he said: "There is scant evidence to tie

Saddam to terrorist organizations and even less to September 11 attacks. Indeed Saddam's goals have little in common with the terrorists who threaten us. There is little incentive for him to make common cause with them. He is unlikely to risk his investment in weapons of mass destruction, much less his country, by handing such weapons to terrorists who would leave Baghdad as the return address.") Scowcroft was not alone. Ex-President Bush (Sr.) and many others also didn't agree. [2-183] Ultimately, it was left to General Abizaid to somehow connect the Pentagon military with the Pentagon civilians. In that role he was notably unsuccessful. The civilians won.

President Bush II declared that his guidance came from a "higher authority" The "higher authority" evidently got it wrong. At a time when the relations between the Secretary of Defense and the Department of Defense were, to put it mildly, at their lowest ebb, the country went to war. We had a plan for the attack but no plan whatever for the aftermath of the war. The administration felt such a plan was unnecessary.

An internal Army War College summary listed the following basic requirements:

1. Large numbers of Iraqi security forces able to support the occupation

2. The international community be willing to pick up the slack from the U.S.
3. An Iraqi government able to quickly spring into being permitting a fast handoff.

None of these conditions pertained but in the argument between the civilian and the military, the civilian spokesman didn't see why it should take more troops to occupy the country than to take down the regime.The campaign was built on capturing Baghdad rather than occupying the country. General Frank concluded that his civilian bosses— Rumsfield, Wolfowitz, Feith, etc., simply lacked the capability to discuss Iraq in practical terms. In order to effect a compromise, Frank came up with a plan (under duress) based on assumptions, most which turned out to be wrong.

As an example in Fallujah, where there was a roster of residents, the military knew the names of virtually all the residents who had volunteered for suicide missions, but the protocol required them to ignore potential perpetrators, and instead find the WMD's. The notion of an insurgency evidently never occurred to the pentagon. (Two former secretaries of defense, James Schlesinger and Harold Brown, were startled by the ("lack of mental agility at the Pentagon") Indeed, the lack of sufficient numbers of troops even left known ammunition dumps and other valuable sites unguarded (and later sacked by the insurgents) and even more significantly, left all borders totally unattended.

Naturally, there were insufficient troops to do police work in the cities since the U.S. military was busy running down WMD's that did not exist. The insurgents clearly could never beat the U.S. military so they attacked civilians with I.E.D.'s and other increasingly sophisticated explosives with little if any response from the Iraqi "police" force. By the time the U.S. was finally forced to recognize that the enemy had changed tactics, the fatalities among our forces rose alarmingly. The Pentagon then listed only our own losses, while ignoring the Iraqi civilian losses —many times our own. The Pentagon described our fatalities as typical of a police action. In fact, if any American city had police losses in the vicinity of 1000 per month, the national guard would be called out.

The decision to invade Iraq may turn out to be one of those historic decisions which lend greatness to political figures. Certainly, Winston Churchill's decision to fight the Nazis single handedly, if necessary was one such choice. The shear courage and tenaciousness of that action united the entire free world behind him –particularly the United States. However, George W. Bush's virtual unilateral invasion of Iraq does not appear to be in a similar vein. We probably won't know the answer to that riddle for generations to come. For the moment we have lost all of our justifications synchronously with our incursion.

1. We charged them with having huge supplies of chemical weapons and forced our own troops to wear specialized clothing. We never found any significant quantities of useable chemical weapons.
2. We charged them with possession of nuclear weapons. Indeed, the Vice President announced that he knew where they were hidden.. We never found any of those either.
3. We claimed that they were trying to buy Uranium ore in Africa. There was no record of any such attempt.
4. We accused them of an active nexus with Al Qaeda. Not a shred of evidence was ever found to support even a casual contact with Al Qaeda.. Indeed, the evidence that did show up indicated that secular Iraqi and the ultrareligious insurgents were very close to being adversaries. The bottom line is that we had them totally contained at a total cost of under two billion dollars a year, and at least that far, no loss of American lives.

5. We were told that we would be greeted as "liberators" with flowers in the streets. Instead, we encountered IED's aimed at us.
6. We were told that the "war" would cost the U.S. less than 1.5 billion dollars. It has already cost us over 300 billion and the final outlook is for a one trillion dollar price tag.
7. The administration claimed that many would join us as they recognized their stake in the fight. Instead, we have lost the U.N., NATO, the E.U. and every single one of our allies including the penultimate one, the United Kingdom.

There were many mistakes made even before this war. For instance, after the apparent victory of the gulf war, we assumed that Saddam Hussein was so weak, he would fall without outside involvement for which reason we refused to help the Kurds and Shiites' rebellion. Their revolt became a disaster with the U.S. as the betrayer. The Shiites, who are our supposed clients during this war have a long tribal memory for betrayals like that.

Americans have usually won wars. (I'm not talking about justifications – only facts after hostilities had begun for whatever justification.) We have never succeeded in "changing regimes". Look at Grenada, Kosovo and Bosnia, and probably eventually even Kuwait and Saudi Arabia as well as all the others. We might well have taken a lesson from all of the European effort during the Crusades, more recently the British in Iraq in the '20s, the French in Algeria and Vietnam, as well as our own prior efforts around the world.

The fact is we did unseat Hussein in a matter of days. It wasn't even a contest. We had better equipment, and better leadership. (Just for comparison, the Iranians couldn't do it in years) We might have regained some good will by departing quickly and leaving behind a Marshal Plan type of operation to at least compensate for all of the damage. That we failed to do so is a reflection of our confusion of purpose and of execution when we attacked Iraq. In fact, we didn't take advantage of opportunities when they occurred. For example, during early 2004 we were actually winning the conflict in Anbar to the extent that the Sunnis were letting out peace feelers. Our confusion of purpose prevented us from reaching out to them (as we did later in the war when we weren't winning) in an early effort to placate the religious antagonists. Even a basic effort to treat prisoners humanely which might have made "crossing over" more attractive to the Sunnis was squandered.

That "war" quickly turned into an insurgency. Armies fight wars, not insurgencies. To win a war, your purpose is to destroy the enemy. That is the textbook way you lose against an insurgency. (For a single example, against sniper fire, a single Marine contingent fired thirty five or more artillery shells plus an estimated thirty thousand rounds from rifles and machine guns) The intent in fighting an insurgency is to diminish physical violence and infrastructural damage in order to minimize civil disarray. We should have never gone into Iraq, but in having gone in, there should have been a plan for unintended consequences –like staying. Such a plan never developed. Instead, we set up an ad hoc series of corrupt and ineffective American bureaucracies to administer a largely disrupted society.

No one actually knew what his job was, much less was trained for it. No civilian stays long enough to do a job even if they would understand the assignment – average civilian job residence is less than a single year giving them neither the chance to reach out to the local population nor to be of any help if they were so inclined. No one knew who was in charge nor who was responsible with the result that no one assumed responsibility for any purported program.

The confusion defeated much of our technological advantage. The CIA, the State Department, the DOD, all have people in Iraq, most of whom don't know which agency pays their salary. In 2003, CALL (Center for Army Lessons Learned) sent a team to Iraq to review our "procedures". This almost completely Republican group reported that virtually all of the intelligence personnel whom they interviewed were young officers and enlisted men, literally none of whom had any intelligence training or analytical skills. Most were waiting to be rotated home with the result that they rarely if ever ventured beyond the Green line and never cultivated any local sources. They are expected to generate at least 120 reports a day and actually produce about thirty, mostly composed of institutional pap which supports the rosiest of outlooks. (Almost all are civilians who can be fired for being "pessimistic".) In addition to failures of initial information, we didn't understand the culture. We had almost no linguists who understood Farsi and didn't trust the loyalties of the local people who did. We didn't even understand the ambitions of the anti-Baathist underground who were our purported allies.

Since the men in the field are largely "fighting blind" they tend to respond to information of almost any kind with massive cordon and sweep operations (NYTimes) where they detain thousands of civilians, the majority of whom merely live in the area, and who then leave our detention as our enemies. All of that is the precise, textbook way to lose hearts and loyalties. I am often teased about WWII, but I can tell you that with all the mistakes of that one, we did it a lot better.

The groups assigned to "reconstruction" weren't in much better shape. Three different investigations have demonstrated that we were overcharged for virtually every item used. The construction personnel were in the main young and inexperienced, Their major "qualification" for the work was in the nature of Republican campaigning. In many cases their introduction to and subsequent understanding of the work was so ill defined that they literally never saw the job site before going home (usually in three months). Administrator Bremer, who somehow was in overall charge of even such small details as a home "reconstruction" would call periodic meetings, ask for reports as to any special difficulties and, receiving negative answers from the young people, would adjourn the meeting. Relations with the military were even worse, if that's possible.

Just as an aside, the president having officially declared victory from the deck of a ship, this post-victory era of some three years [*as of this writing–ed.*] is estimated as costing the U.S., at an absolute minimum, over 350 billion dollars with absolutely no end in sight and no formal way of paying for that burden. The cost in toto has been forecast by the Congressional Budget Office (CBO) at over two trillion dollars so while lots of people are working on the elimination of the "death tax", the birth tax to our children, grandchildren, and great grandchildren might well exceed $300,000 each. Of course, that does not include the costs of rebuilding Iraq and recompensing victims of collateral damage when we actually do "win". Indeed the real threat of this war could conceivably end up being not defeat, but either national bankruptcy or severe cuts in social services like Social Security, Medicare, the environment, the road system, police and fire departments, etc.

As a matter of fact, the American people have never been given any actual description of the term "winning". It would have be something of a miracle if the insurgency had not formed and once formed, gotten worse as a consequence of mistakes, bad policies, bad planning, and incredible ignorance. There was no food, water, sewage disposal, jobs, or even shops, not to mention hospitals, schools, fire departments, police departments, etc. It all kind of reminds me of the fact that our state department located and saved the Japanese plans for bombing Pearl Harbor after the war. Up until the day the bombs were dropped, Japanese plans were painfully detailed down to the number of times the sailors were permitted to bathe.

For the time starting with the return of the Pearl Harbor attack fleet, there was very little having to do with the U.S. Apparently, they expected the Americans to go home. After laughing at the Japanese naiveté for 62 years, we did precisely the same thing in Iraq.

In 2004, the Pentagon military, more realistic than their civilian counterparts, requested a summary review of what was wrong. (Some of the problems were already pretty well established. An Army War College study stated unequivocally that the "insurgency in Iraq is expanding and becoming more deadly as a consequence of U.S. policy." The Cato Institute came to the conclusion that any extended American military presence in Iraq would be a disaster for the U.S.) General Casey hired Kalev Sepp, a retired Special Forces officer with a resume too long to detail. Boiled down his chart listed nine unsuccessful characteristics of our effort:

1. the focus on responses to the insurgency
2. the failure to engage the population
3. over sized operations
4. the preponderance of large protection bases
5. inappropriate use of special forces
6. low priority assigned to advisor selection
7. low priority assigned to indigenous force training

8. no priority assigned to building a peacetime governmental process
9. open borders, airspace, and coastlines

Looking at this list leads one to conclude that all of the above are, and should have been, post-war preplanned operations. The only test of military performance is winning or losing wars. They won the war. The civilians of the White House, the Congress and the Pentagon, at this point, appear to have lost the peace and in the process, compromised the valued authority of American moral leadership of the world.

What should have additionally been considered is the ultimate financial cost of the war— a factor which has been swamped by the mind numbing running price of the war. The total cost of the Gulf war, which we actually did win in terms of intentions and goals, is not often calculated into the publicized totals. For example, of the approximate 600,000 soldiers who participated in that war, over 150,000 are still on medical disability ten years later.

The abnormally high incidence of cancer among the veterans is now being traced to the depleted uranium shells that were in common usage during the tank battles. Indeed the incidence of hysterectomies and birth defects among the veterans and their wives is similarly out of the statistical bounds for their age group. Most of the veterans refused to admit any psychiatric problems although a DOD survey estimated that as many as two thirds of those who were positive for PTSD were not being treated.

It has been declared that due to the participation of so many allies, the U.S. actually "made a profit" from the Gulf War. None of the above was added into "the books" for that P/L estimate, nor has the running costs of the engagement since then.

It is worth repeating that bankruptcy is the real dilemma of all empires, not victory or defeat. Bankruptcy defeated the Romans, the British, the French, the Russians, and even the Germans. The Iraq war is the first major war the U.S. engaged in which was not a reaction to an attack on us. We now have an estimated 9 trillion dollar ten-year deficit less than a half dozen years after a 4 trillion dollar surplus. The causes will no doubt be argued for many years but it is beyond argument that the current cost of the Iraqi occupation is running between 10 and 20 million dollars an hour and growing 24/7. Some wars are unavoidable and cost can't be a factor in waging them. This was a war of choice. The administration claimed that the ultimate cost would be under 1.5 billion dollars and would be paid for with Iraqi oil.

The war is far from over and the real figure is already an underestimate by over 27,000 percent. This time we have only the British for allies and they are pulling out during the current year regardless of the situation on the ground.

And finally, everyone knows that the greatest power on earth is being fought successfully enough to raise public questions concerning whether the fight is worth the cost. We have the most advanced, sophisticated, trained and equipped army in history. The truth is that we won the "war" in four days against an army which the Iranians could not beat in four years. How can we be defeated against those odds? It seems to me that the answer to the question of defeat is more simple than the obverse question of victory. We pit a 60 million dollar tank against their $600 explosive. We fight their grenade launchers with expensive airplanes and helicopters. Our expensive infrared-aimed rifles fight their cheap Kalashnikov rifles. We pit our technology against their hit and run tactics. Indeed, the Ottomon Empire, which can charitably be characterized as crude, very nearly defeated the great British Empire during WWI. And even after "peace" was declared, these are the same people who fought off the British in Iraq in the '20s and '30s, the French during that same time period, and the Russians (during the '90s) in Afghanistan under pretty much the same circumstances with pretty much the same tactics. It is said that the definition of insanity is repeating the same tactics and expecting different results. So for all of that, technology doesn't really explain the results.

Vice President Cheney notwithstanding, there is no longer any debate over adjectives for describing events in Iraq. If Al Qaeda wasn't there before the war, it's there now. People infiltrating the borders from Saudi Arabia, Iran, Syria, and even Turkey are producing an insurgency infinitely worse than was there before the invasion. If the current situation in Iraq is not a civil war, few – left or right – want to see further American involvement and the major question is how to get out without exacerbating the entire Middle East roil. Security is dwindling with casualties and destruction of property already worse than ever and rising. The violence has already spread to Lebanon with both Saudi Arabia and Jordan becoming measurably more vulnerable every day. Even our "model" victory in Afghanistan is once again very shaky with the President demanding an increase in American troops. The Iranians, a Gilbert and Sullivan army before the Iraq war are now a major player in the area with our ability to take them on so compromised that even the Israelis, still lacking a peace at home, are liable to be sucked into violence in Iran.

It is easy to blame nations or peoples for the debacle and there is certainly lots of blame to go around, but in our part of the world the man in charge is the man in charge and there is no doubt as to who that might be. If there is a way out, it isn't obvious, and failing to find one will inevitably imply the end of American leadership, certainly in the Middle East, as we saw the end of European control there after WWI. Such a failure would completely undermine any American "posture" and further erode European support for a Jewish state, already in question. It will justify independent action by France, Russia, Japan, China, North Korea, Iran, Saudi Arabia, Egypt, and all the others. As if all of that were insufficient, the Sunni's, the Shia, and most likely the Kurds as well, will likely split into separate communities after a very bloody ethnic cleansing campaign. Possibly worst of all, the likelihood is that the world, lacking a military superpower, will remilitarize as it did after the collapse of the British Empire with the cost in blood, treasure and the environment almost too horrifying to envision

There is actually no dearth of "plans" none of which have happy outlooks. The most obviously unacceptable proposal is "stay the course" which even this President now rejects. Another is to split Iraq into three independent, separate states, namely Sunni in the west, Shia in the east and Kurdish in the north. With this plan one can count on countries such as Saudi Arabia and Egypt becoming involved to protect the Sunni's, Turkey becoming involved to prevent a Kurdish state, and the Iranians becoming involved to expand Shia dominance in the area. Neither of these is likely to happen if for no other reason then the resulting blood bath and fear of the flood of Iraqi refugees into neighboring Arab states. The Israeli war is 60 years in the past and the refugees from that war have yet to be "naturalized" in their countries of refuge. The Arabs don't want a repeat of more millions of other Muslims with the same script.

It seems as though the only real choices for the U.S. are all withdrawal in one guise or another. The only question remaining is how to do it with minimal damage to our troops, and to our international position. Even the President himself, whose divine inspiration initiated this astonishing blunder, now favors Iraqi "performance-based withdrawal" starting with a probably inadequate so-called U.S. troop "surge," and still without any rational strategy for departure in the very likely event of performance disappointment. It would seem to many observers to be a change in nomenclature but the same failed policy. Even at this early stage, the "troops" supplied by the Iraqis are already 50% undermanned as reported by our own NSA–hardly an optimistic forecast. The quandry of this approach is that we are putting the American lives and reputation in the hands of a splintered Arab state with very little modern record to report accomplishment and a great deal to report failure. It is the fourth variation of the same plan after three prior failures so the question is not desirability but feasibility.

Another option is immediate withdrawal which, in the real world, most likely varies from the President's "plan" only in terms of schedule. If an ensuing area-wide bloodbath defeated "our side" this choice might validate the righteousness of Sunni Islamic behavior in the eyes of God because victory in battle is, as always, the proof positive of Allah's pleasure. At the very least, it would enhance the impression that third-rate powers can defeat first-rate powers. It would undoubtedly undermine our international credibility as a "power" and as an even-handed mediator. If the Iraqi army failed on the ground, the consequences in the Middle-East would be generations in recovering

The third scheme is a calendar-based withdrawal which is independent of Iraqi performance. Making this choice would be based on the judgment that there will never come a day in which Iraqi army presence will permit U.S. army absence. Failure on the ground would have precisely the same bloody result as failure of the performance-based plan. If, in the face of impending Iraqi defeat or of Middle East chaos, we don't withdraw, this would immediately evolve into the President's plan. If we do withdraw in those circumstances, then it is exactly like the unconditional plan. In any case, all of these strategies will encourage "go it alone" adventurism for any state, Islamic or non-Islamic alike.

In any case, as General Powell forecast, we broke it without much help so we can fix it unaided. Whatever the road out is, there is every likelihood that we, the United States, will end up paying for human reparations, and the repair of the roads, buildings, education system, economic system, water system, police, military, fire and environmental systems for generations to come –all without help. None of that was figured into Mr. Cheney's 1.5 billion dollar cost of war estimate.

Finally, I think it is imperative to recognize that there are people who are more anxious to die for religious theology than the West is for political ideology. It has been a long experience for them. The Moslem religion is central to their being, the ultimate basis of focus, identity and loyalty. For them the defeat of Islam can only mean that they are not practicing Islam correctly. This, in spite of the Sunni/Shia split.

The Sunni's believe that what is, is right. The community is God's community. To the Shia, all Islamic government since the murder of Ali has been illegitimate which makes all existing order illegitimate. The difference might seem trivial but the two have been fighting each other for fourteen centuries with that as the principal excuse. It would be simple to blame poverty for such a record but the fact is that the young men who blew up the London subways were middle class typical Brits. The men who flew into the Twin towers were mostly educated middle class.

It seems more likely to me that the culprit here is not religious extremism but religion itself. They believe in a heaven to which they could take a short cut by martyrdom. They believe in a heaven where they would find seventy-two "virgins" waiting for them after martyrdom (which always makes me think there must be a shortage of virgins in their heaven.) They believe in a God who was omnipresent and watching, who empowered them to sacrifice untold millions of lives across the centuries to accomplish their purpose. They believe in a divine rule book which ultimately approves of sending their brothers and sisters, even their children, out to sacrifice themselves in order to defeat nonbelievers. They are convinced that the certainty of a single ancient book outweighed that of thousands of books, over thousands of years of human observation and experience. They believe that their confidence is the only truth and all others are false. That is what they were taught from childhood with no chance to compare and evaluate relative merit and no choice of parenting. Faith is the ingredient underlying their successes against overwhelming odds and faith is the culprit because it brooks no argument and accepts no challenge. Faith encourages the suppression of proof of a sun-centered universe, and the arrest of a teacher who merely suggests evolution as an alternate story of origins. Faith eventually permits any atrocity because faith is always "inspired". Faith is their stealthy weapon. It may be powerful but it's no secret.

SOURCES

Among many others

[1] *Out of Iraq* –George McGovern and William R. Polk
[2] *Fiasco* – Thomas E. Ricks
[3] *Worse Than Watergate* – John Dean
[4] *A Peace to End All Peace* – David Fromkin
[5] *Islam And The West* – Bernard Lewis
[6] *The God Delusion* – Richard Dawkins
[7] (Article in *Newsweek*, Jan.8, 2007) *The New Middle East* – Richard N. Haase
[8] (Article in *YaleGlobal* 10/31/06) *The Withdrawal Syndrome* –Part I – Richard N. Haase
[9] www.mideastweb.org – A brief History of Israel and Palestine and the Conflict – Ami Isseroff

MARTIN J. BLICKSTEIN

Martin J. Blickstein (1925-2007) had a long career in technology as an engineer, businessman, salesman, consumer and observer. He participated in the transformation into a digital world. After retiring from full time engagement in business he continued to study trends in world affairs and taught courses in current events. He is the author of *Anticipating Tomorrow: Living and Making a Living in the 21st Century* (iUniverse, 2004).

Printed in the United States
149521LV00001B/10/P